Writers of the Aether

A Writers' Rooms Community Anthology

Erin Casey, ed.

All rights and copyright of individual works reserved by the authors of their piece.

All rights and copyright of this book in its entirety reserved by The Writers' Rooms.

All characters, events, and narratives presented in this book are fictional: any resemblance to reality is a matter of coincidence.

First edition, 2021.
The Writers' Rooms
Iowa City, IA
welcome@thewritersrooms.org

Cover design is by Skylar Alexander Moore. Art is public domain: "Aurora Borealis" by Étienne Léopold Trouvelot.

ISBN: 978-0-578-85675-9

To the writers of the community who make
The Writers' Rooms possible…thank you.

Table Of Contents

Introduction from the Publishing Committee..1
Author Biographies..3
But is it Art by G.Z. Chapman..7
Air of Impermanence by Kelli Ann Brommel...............8
Chimes by Madeleine Kleppinger....................................11
Teach Me How to Breathe by Erin Casey......................24
Finding Breath by J.E. Brooke..27
The Breaking of Air by Steven Torriano Berry..........31
Glass Houses by J.E. Brooke..37
The Breath by Laura Goldman Weinberg....................49
The Butterfly, the Tornado, and the Sailboat by Derek Maurer..52
About The Writers' Rooms...59

Introduction

Dear Reader, thank you for your support of The Writers' Rooms (TWR)! By picking up this book, you have made your first step into joining our community as a whole. This book is our way to celebrate you and to thank everyone for helping our dream of the Rooms come to life.

TWR is an organization which endeavors to create a safe, inclusive community for all writers. We believe that everyone has a wealth of knowledge and a story to share. In our Rooms we bring both to the table. These community-led meetings include a myriad of craft discussions, prompts, lessons, and time to write. Our events, which are usually held in conjunction with local businesses and libraries, offer a safe space in which to meet other members of your local writing community. Due to COVID-19, our Rooms have gone virtual for the time being in hopes of providing a place for writers to express themselves.

Our Rooms would not exist were it not for the incredible writers throughout the creative corridor. We've watched new writers learn from seasoned minds. Authors with writer's block have found a way to flourish and venture into their literary world once again. Most importantly, people have found a Room to call home, a place where they feel safe to share their voice and find help when they struggle.

The stories, poetry, and non-fiction you're about to read are from our community. We are writers helping writers who endeavor to share each others' voices. We chose the theme of air for this anthology to continue your elemental journey.

Just remember, no matter where you are in your writing journey, you are never alone. You have a community waiting for you.

Best,
Erin Casey, Ross T. Byers,
Derek Maurer, and G.Z. Chapman

Author Biographies

G. Z. Chapman writes fun fiction drawing from his life in mechanics, agriculture, restaurant & bar, programming, plumbing, business, consulting, writing, and devouring fiction, comics, and Wikipedia.

Kelli Ann Brommel sometimes participates in local poetry slams and Golden Attic meetings. Three of her poems have been accepted for publication in various formats. Kelli Ann is an empty nest mother who once taught grade school. She started a graduate program in the fall of 2020, hoping to begin a second career in librarianship.

Author Biographies

Madeleine Kleppinger is a scientist by day, writer by night. Her written works include a drafted historical fiction novel, short stories, and a blog www.mkleppinger.com for helping readers discover their greatest story. Some of her favorites are people, Sonnet the American Bulldog, and fresh carafes of coffee.

Erin Casey is an urban fantasy writer and author of The Purple Door District series. An advocate for mental health, she also writes about struggling with depression and anxiety. She's an avid bird mom and a lover of all things fantasy. You can learn more about her at erincasey.org.

Author Biographies

J. E. Brooke is a public health anthropologist by day, fantasy writer by night. When she isn't writing stories and novels about mermaids and dragons, she can be found knitting or cross stitching, cooking delicious food, or lost in the pages of a good book. She lives in Iowa City.

Steven Torriano Berry is an award-winning independent filmmaker who has created and executive produced the anthology series Black Independent Showcase, and, Black Visions/Silver Screen: Howard University Student Film Showcase for WHUT-TV 32, in Washington, D.C. He is co-creator and director of Noh Matta Wat, the first dramatic television series of Belize, Central America, and director of "Livin' Mi Life," the first episodic sit-com of Belize.

Author Biographies

Laura Goldman Weinberg is multi-talented and multi-creative. Her art, songs, and writings are universal, recognizing the oneness everywhere. She allows the creative energy to flow through her and continues to create in various forms with the hope of inspiring and uplifting others.

Derek Maurer of Iowa City is proud to have attended the first Violet Realm session and most of the them since. He also is co-concierge of the Parchment Lounge open writing group. After an unremarkable career in journalism, PR, and marketing, he turned to fiction and is still working on novel No. 1. His essay for this volume, "The Butterfly, the Tornado, and the Sailboat," marks a return to that form after many years of essay-idleness. He enjoys sailing and, together with his wife Linda, also music, camping, hiking, and easy bike trails.

But is it Art
G. Z. Chapman

Not often do the elements congregate—they tend not to mix. When they do interact, thoughts exchange and the world sees change.

"You two are not really going to have this most creative elemental argument again are you? It really burns me up."

Air smiled, not even bothering to mention how much Fire needed her. "I once ripped a brick wall off a sorority, grabbed the sheet off the bed while leaving everything else untouched inside the room, then tied the sheet in a bow on the tree outside."

The smooth and fluid voice of Water seemed to fill all the lower space. "Nice, but I think true creativity can only be subtle. I once took a sash in the wash and twisted it into a multitude of knots, none of them the same. I finished with a Gordian Knot. No matter how the humans tugged or how the knot was moved, they could not find the end. They finally cut it, ending the magic, leaving two pieces of a sash."

Air pondered Water's comment. Gordian Knots. Subtle. Air then rushed away towards a large human city near many lakes. Several long-haired humans had just exited a building, patting each other's and their own long hair.

Perfect.

Air of Impermanence
Kelli Ann Brommel

The things to which we are heir
Cedar chest stacked neatly with
Dish towels and serving spoons
Today full of papers and plaques
Baby's department store photo shoot
In the closet
Cardboard box of broken jewelry, deck of cards,
A jingling genie bottle with coins from
Places never visited
Wheat pennies and buffalo nickels
Plastic tub of farmhouse journals
Black and white portraits come loose from
Their sticky corners
Military hat at the same jaunty angle
As Grandpa's smile a
Swiss goatherd's bell
Walking stick
Steamer
It's all yours now ere
The down-sizing boomer estates became nil they
Were emptied of
Hand-tatted doilies and the
Careful, ancient crafts you must
Admire, put away, save

Writers of the Aether

Imagine yourself Jane Eyre
Who had nothing, then something,
Her gain bittersweet
Accept your position as
Keeper of special collections
Curator of the Family Museum
Whose founders stare back at you
Begging remembrance
At this duty you err
Feeling stifled as you do
By too many things, the
Bombarding echo of voices
The vases, the stacks, the boxes, the books
Who will take the things
If you do not
Who will remember
If you do not

Where is the evidence of human existence
If not in the things we once used
Some future archeologist will
Unearth those bronzed booties and declare
That we valued childhood
That we loved our children
The future will make what it will of the landfill
The basement shelves
The honeycombed complexes crammed to the rafters
With all that we
Thought we needed

Air of Impermanence

The things to which we are heir
Will become air
Like us, breaking down
Long after we have turned to ash,
To soil, to fertilizer, into
Cosmic particles begging to recollect
To be recollected
What else can we do when
Even these words
Now imprinted or written on a cloud
Might disappear
Might have no one left to read them

But there's the gamble
The mortal hope that someone
If not a daughter or son or nephew or niece
Just somebody, anybody will
Own the object of our lives
Will save it in a box and take it out
To hold
And we will live again
If only in that moment, in those hands
Greedy as we are
To not have lived in vain
To not have been something, then nothing,
Our gain bittersweet

Chimes
Madeleine Kleppinger

I stare at the six wind chimes on the rack. Two are duplicates. The one-of-a-kind designs make me want to pick them, just because then there will be an empty hook on the shelf. Proof I shopped at the Wood Barn and Lawn today.

Leaving my house is hard. Being out in public is easier, except for the stares when I do weird stuff like buying lots of wind chimes. I don't even try to say they're gifts anymore. When I get up to the counter, I will slap down my card to pay, my name says the rest. Allyson Leeder, town survivor.

Some news stories called me a survivor. Others, a victim. One even wrote "dead girl", before the editor sent condolences and apologized for his fired freelancer. When I didn't reply, they sent flowers to the house.

I'm just a person who wanted to live. Any person with survival instincts would've done, or tried to do, what I did. The body refuses to die; it chokes the brain before it'll suffocate the lungs.

Did you know that? Your brain starves to death before the lungs and heart?

I learned that reading about suicide.

I take the longest woodstock chime, because it's an elephant and leaves a space on the shelf almost the shape of me crouched over. The bamboo pipes dangling are the elephant's legs and trunk. The carvings on the center bulb are the eyes, mouth, and ears. None of my other fifty-seven wind chimes look like this one. I flip the price tag with my thumb: $32.50.

Add it to their tab. The charges they rack up on my life. The cost of total ruin, that no one saves money for.

How could I have known home break-ins, tortures, and homicides aren't covered by homeowner's insurance? Or by medical insurance? Or by anyone if the suspects are never arrested and convicted? Yep, that all comes out of my wallet. Hospital bills, window repairs, axed dry wall replacement, and this dumb wind chime fetish.

My parents keep trying to ward me off spending through my savings, but I kind of hope running out of money will snap me out of it. Like hunger will make me want to go back to work. And the electricity being turned off will make me want to reemerge into civilization.

I think I'm going to hang my new elephant over my juniper shrub, near the bathroom window. The shrub my dad insisted on planting to keep burglars from looking in my window, checking for things to steal while I was out. The shrub I scraped my cheek and ear on trying to hide.

My therapist suggested twice I move out of my house and live somewhere new, and with a roommate. Everyone suggests a roommate, like I was proof girls shouldn't live alone. But no matter how screwed up in the head I am, I won't leave my home. The little house I bought with my first savings account for the down payment. It's tucked at the end of the street, three doors down from the last streetlight. The bricks are smoothed from the years of wind whipping through the mortar channels. I love the white shutters most of all. The white columned, flat, front porch second best. The lawn continues right up to the house. A big welcome mat direct to my front door.

    The previous owners, an older couple who passed in the night clasping each other's hands, left behind hooks around the porch for hanging baskets full of ferns. Three days after I moved in, I hung up a reed wind chime I bought at a market in Thailand my senior year of college.

    The paddle is a carved wooden elephant. And with how my porch faces the Western sky, a breeze always blows by the front of the house. I thought hearing the pipes dong would turn my new place into a retreat, like the mountain monasteries where I'd gone to watch the monks pray and play their instruments. Listening to the slow sound, it still gives me goosebumps. A raised flesh feeling as the sound moves over your arms and around your neck.

    The second chime was added by my mother. She wanted to even out the aesthetic, a chime on each side. But hers clangs metal pipes and glass beads like a Goodwill bag full of thrown out home goods. I'd take it down on the days I knew she wouldn't pop by for a visit and notice it missing. It made migraines and hangovers worse. Her wind chime was up the night they came, and I've never taken it down since. The clanking gave him away.

Chimes

I listen long enough to know the sounds that are only wind and not predators stalking my windows. And since I can't stop hearing the wind chimes in my head, I have to hear them in real life. To assure myself I am still alive and not going mental.

The new elephant is around the corner from my first elephant. I'm oddly satisfied by the number fifty-eight. More than halfway to a hundred, a respectable collection.

The day my mom brought me home from the hospital, my neighbors had cleaned up the glass and rehung my wind chimes. Mom thought they were being nosy, getting as close to a murder scene as they ever would. But then two days later, a lady up the block dropped off flowers and a small hummingbird feeder with tinkling metal bars hanging below. Her cursive scrawl on the card, *I hope the music of your life can resume soon. Call if you need anything.*

I needed someone on July twenty-seventh.

My therapist is helping me work through the blame, though. We say it together, "The accident was late at night. My house is far down the street. I was knocked unconscious before I could scream. People would have helped me if they knew."

But I did scream. I screamed so loud I damaged a vocal cord. I cut the sides of my mouth with the gag trying to bite through it. I knocked every piece of furniture over while I tried to run away. July twenty-seventh was the loudest night of my life.

They came like cymbals, crashing my peace into shattered fragments, right near my ears. Those monsters were a crescendo of tasteless music, wrecking my mind. Whipping wind in leaves. Branches knocking one another. Metal trash cans bumping against aluminum siding. Chimes clanging against shoulders.

I told the police a really tall man hit my wind chimes, every time he circled the house, like he was announcing his coming. He bumped into the pipes the first time he unlocked the screen door. He knocked some glass beads when he climbed from the back bedroom window.

The other two were smaller, maybe women or teenagers. It was hard to believe they just knocked into things like he did. The police questioned me for the motive over and over, but I spent long, intimate hours with those creeps. They hadn't come for my tv or Mac, they came for the simple pleasure of hurting someone who would be afraid.

That isn't a sensible answer for a small-town police force, though. Jealousy, adultery, hatred. Those were the M-Os they were hoping for.

You know what else didn't seem right? I never saw their faces. They wore masks the whole time, even after they thought I was dead. They kept the cheapy, plastic Halloween masks on while they cleaned up prints and left the house. Maybe I was spared a nightmare though. Like, how many people in public look like a Halloween mask? Chances are way slimmer I'd have to see that than a tall brute with dark eyebrows. Anyways, I've named them, in order to cope with the reality that people hurt people and what happened to me was not some phantom, ghost thing.

Chimes

So the Big One, he moved the slowest but never stopped coming after me. I pleaded with him, before he thumped my lights out. He made the wind chimes clang together to warn me of my doom. He wanted me to be afraid of him. He needed me to quake before his footsteps even sounded in my ears.

I put them up in front of every window and door, high and low, trying to catch an unexpectant shoulder passing by too close to my house. I figured if the guy that intruded into my home that night could give himself away by clattering into my wind chime, then I'd protect myself, the next time.

There are black ones and wooden ones that you can't see at night unless you shine a flashlight right on them. I've tethered a few with fishing line to the ground so they will clank if a foot catches.

My therapist says I don't have to stop buying wind chimes, but I've got to stop relying on them for my protection. Bad things could still happen to me. She always says, as I leave her office, "Allyson, you are safe now. No one is going to hurt you anymore."

I might believe her, if they'd caught the people who did this to me. The people who cut me and burned me and beat me. I watched money exchanged from one hand to another through slits in my swollen, puffed up eyelids. They could have been repaying each other soda money or taking bets on how long I could withstand the punishment before passing out again. The wind chimes stay.

It's not worth asking why. Not any more than it is worth depending on a dumb lawn ornament to save your life. I heard them come in and still couldn't save myself. Bad people exist and while I lay there in my own blood I listened to the songs of the Thai monks outside and believed I would live. My body wouldn't let me give up.

And when I woke up in the hospital room and I had lived, I wanted to hear every ting and clang and gong and bang and ring ever. Sounds in my ears mean I lived and keep living. Sound waves come toward me, affirming my pulse and breath and nerves firing. I drop glass bowls. Unscrew the metal shower curtain rod and bang it on the side of the bathtub. I throw keys down on concrete steps. Noises mean life.

I promised my parents this week I would apply for one job. I had a really good one before, the tech coordinator for the high school. I purchased laptops and uploaded software and found cool programs for teachers to use in classrooms. Plus, I was good at it. Everyone knew this small town needed to move into the 2010s, so it was an important job, too.

My new job will probably be behind a computer, though. Meetings and people and power point presentations, too much would be relying on me to keep it together. I kick myself for not understanding people who seemed like slobs to me before this. I thought mental toughness just stuck with you, even after a Saw movie scene. But they changed me. Knowing someone can exert that much control changed me. Most nights, I can't decide on dinner. I don't make plans with friends. I sit, listening to the stupid wind chimes, planning what I would've done different.

Chimes

It's loud as crap outside tonight. Perfect weather to stay inside and freak out. My MacBook shines bright and there sit my seventy unclosed tabs. Websites I like. Purchases I plan to make. Possible job opportunities. There is a company seeking freelance web designers. The ad boasts work from home, great benefits, and flexible scheduling. When I click on the post, the pay isn't bad either. I shoot my resume off just as the windows creak and groan from the thrashing wind outside.

Clash. BANG. Ting, ting, clank.

The storm is just beginning and already my collection is getting ripped apart outside. My cellphone rings loud.

"Hey sweetie, it's Mom. Want Dad to come get you? Storm is going to get pretty loud, TV says a possible flash flood warning."

"Nah, I'll be alright. I don't want Dad out driving in this. What if a tree branch comes down or he hydroplanes?"

"Nonsense, Allyson. I can hear him already getting his coat on. I've got the guest room all made up. Bring your laptop and you can work from here."

She wants to protect me, I get it, but I really want to stay home right now. I want to be around my things, locked inside my house, waiting out the storm.

"Mom, my wind chimes are blowing everywhere. I need to go get them down. Tell Dad not to come, I'll be fine."

I hang up before she can say, "Forget those damn wind chimes," or "Stop being irrational," or "Allyson, we can't sleep knowing you are still living in that house alone."

The air has been hot and humid today. It is either going to turn into a twister or rain cats and dogs. The wind is thrashing my house now. There is no way I can go outside and get all fifty-eight of my wind chimes down. I could rescue a few favorites.

Whoooooo, waaaaahhhh

Tornado sirens blare and howl with the wind. A freaking competition is going on outside, who can yell the loudest. The sky is green beyond my drapes and a deep purple mist is forming on the lawn out front. Dark swirls of moisture magnetize to the storm clouds. Metal pipes rip from strings and scatter across my lawn. Broken bamboo ornaments lay smashed on my concrete sidewalk. A car careens down our block and takes cover in a driveway.

A funnel starts to swirl and I beg the menacing heavens above to make my dad turn around. I hope the thrashing about in the sky convinces him not to come over here after me. My parents' house is way sounder than mine.

Smash, cling.

A small metal triangle is flung from its hook against the siding by the window. The lights flicker off and on and then go out. I dash to get a flashlight, blanket, and my cell phone. Before taking cover, I can't help but check every lock in the house. I secure the back door twice.

WAAAAHHHHHHeeeeee.

The sirens scream out warning. Screw me for not buying a house with a basement. I crouch in the hallway, debating if I should go back and get the new gun in my nightstand.

Chimes

Crash!

Was that a tree branch smashing a window? The air is still around me, so it could've been my car window.

Smack, smack, pow.

When this is over, I won't be surprised if every single one of my wind chimes is blasted to pieces.

Brummmm, crack.

The house goes electric with blue lightning. My vision spots. And then torrents of rain hammer down on the roof. I can't hear the sirens so the twister must've dissolved into buckets of water.

Lying on my side, back pressing against the wall, I listen to the washing outside. Sprays of water coat my house. For about an hour, the water showers the earth.

Swoosh, putt, plunk. Drip, drop.

The storm is passing over. I crawl to a drape and lift up a corner and a ray of evening sun lands on my cheek. Outside the damage is incredible. Shingles ripple up on rooftops like waves. Windshields crack into spider web formations. Heavy branches sag from ancient neighborhood trees, fresh wood bright in its new exposure.

My wind chimes lay like exploded firework casings after the Fourth of July. Bits of metal and wood and plastic shrapnel dot the wet grass.

Bile rises up in my throat. I race outside to pick up pieces, my hands collecting remnants of my own security. I make a pouch with my shirt and start to fill that up. I turn to sprint back to the house for a bag and I see my neighbors looking at the side of their house, smashed in by a felled tree. Down the block, three men are trying to free a woman trapped inside her car.

My house is still intact. Seeing the pieces in my hands and in my shirt, I am still intact. My fingers open and my shirt edge drops letting the garbage sift to the ground again. Grabbing my cell phone out of my pocket, I call Mom.

"Please, Mom, tell me Dad didn't leave the house?" I beg.

"He's okay. He never got a chance to leave. Are you okay?" She asks.

"Ya, Mom, I'm okay. Got to go, my neighbors need help."

This week I applied for three jobs and interviewed for one. I cooked dinner for my parents when they came over, so we didn't have to order pizza again. My neighbors helped me pick up the wind chimes from everywhere and I don't think I am going to fix them. I told my therapist, when I am ready I'll buy one, just one, and put it up on the porch. Right now, I'm enjoying the quiet.

Mom bought me an ambient noise machine; she said my house is too quiet now. Sometimes I'll listen to the babbling brook or car noises. There's one setting, the sound of wind through a cave, but it kind of creeps me out. Like a wooing noise filling an empty space.

Chimes

I'm ready to take up space again, though. Restore normal to my life. I'd like to meet someone, that could be good for me. Like, someone I feel safe around, who helps me sleep through the night.

Ting, clink, crink.

Did I forget to put the box out by the curb, with the trash can? I won't get up early enough to catch the truck in the morning, better go do it now. Grabbing my hoodie, I head to the back door to take out the garbage.

Cling, ding, ting, bing.

Did a cat get in the box of pieces? Ugh, little furball better not be making a mess. How'd the backdoor get open?

Bring, ding. Ting, ting.

One of my old wind chimes, now repaired, is hanging on the hook right outside the opened back door. My eyes shoot down to the box of pieces I set by the curb on the right side of the trash can. The flaps bounce open in the night breeze. Taped to one of the freed edges is a skinny slip of paper.

I am bolted in place to the floor.

The wind chime picks up the tempo of its song and the chill of the breeze snaps me out of it. The paper is soft and tears from the pull of the tape, there is a dampness that could either be night humidity or sweaty palm. I inhale a sharp breath.

Writers of the Aether

Ring, ting, ding
We did a little thing
Clink, clank, clunk,
Your head will go thunk
Shish, shoosh, shush
Keep quiet now, hush
Twang, clang, bang
Gotcha, says the gang

Teach Me How to Breathe
Erin Casey

One phone call on an ordinary day
made me forget how to breathe.
The sun beat down through
windows open just a crack
as his voice crackled through
the speaker of my car.

Three words, nothing more.
Three words that wrapped their hands
around my throat and
plucked the breath from my lungs.
Three words.
"Mom just died."

His voice echoed in my ears.
I raced home to unbury
photo albums covered in dust.
"We need pictures," I rasped,
the only mantra that kept me breathing.
"Mom would want pictures."

Each call to a sister, a brother,
cost another breath.
And when the phone went silent,
I stared at your smiling face,
frozen in time on a glossy card,
my chest aching for relief.

Four months later…
His melancholy voice keeps
me captive in the car again.
I wait for the news
that'll stifle my breath,
but his only utterance
is of a day run afoul.

My mind knows that all's well,
but my body heaves
as if he's stolen my breath again.
Limbs languish in tension and cramps.
My mouth gapes for air
between forced laughter and sympathy.

"No one is dead," I repeat to myself,
an echoed mantra from four months ago
as I tore through your pictures
in albums and dirty frames.
No one is dead.
But my heart doesn't know the difference.

Can you teach me how to breathe again?
To let the cool air fill my lungs
and show me that the world isn't dark?
Can you teach me how to breathe again
so the tears can roll
while I fall apart?

Teach me how to breathe,
so I can see a light burning
at the end of the tunnel
instead of the chill
that awaits me when I
imagine a future without you.

Teach Me How to Breathe

Teach me how to breathe words
back onto the page to share my voice
the way you encouraged me to do.
And help me remove the claws of guilt
tearing through my chest
and threatening to still my creative breath.

One day, each day, seems far away,
so distant without your voice
on the other end of the line.
Without your breathy laugh and
comforting words to remind me
that I will always be loved.

Mom, teach me how to breathe
and loosen the tension in my body.
Spill it out like light through my fingers
the way you taught me when anxiety
overpowered me and tried to rule
my every waking move.

Teach me how to breathe and
know how to move forward
into a new dawn while
you watch me from afar,
adrift on a breeze,
that's never too far from my heart.

Finding Breath
J.E. Brooke

I wake up in the middle of the night in my narrow bed, already gasping for breath. My heart slams itself against my ribs, stomach clenching in sympathy. My body shakes, limbs trembling in tiny spasms I can't control or send away. Part of my sleep-addled brain wonders again if I am dying, even though this has happened before in the last few months and I have survived each time. *What if this is the time you don't?* the morbid part of my brain whispers in the dark. I try not to listen. It helps to focus on something else: the brush of my dorm-room sheets under my fingers, the low hum of the mini-fridge in the corner. Recently, I've started pretending that I'm on a beach somewhere along the north shore of Lake Superior, wind blowing through the autumn-kissed birch trees as I watch the small waves break over the sand. It helps to calm me down, however slowly. Eventually, I will learn to find my breath itself as an anchor, but for now I fight with the invisible monster constricting me.

The last part of me not consumed by the engulfing panic, or trying to mitigate it, is frustrated and angry. It had been a good day, relatively speaking. No exams to worry about, no looming deadlines for papers or other projects on the horizon. I had taken care of myself: eaten good food in the commons, walked around campus for exercise rather than just to get from building to building for class, had even gone to the guided meditation session at lunch, at the risk of falling asleep from being full of food, and closing my eyes in the small, drapery lined Spiritual Life room in the student union. I'm doing well, I tell myself. There's no reason I should be having these attacks, yet here I am: fighting for air and for control over my body. Adding to the mounting frustration is the fact that it will likely take me an hour or more to fall asleep again, and there is no guarantee that this will be my last attack of the night. I will be a zombie in class tomorrow, walking groggily from lecture to lecture, barely hanging on to what I am supposed to be learning, adding to the mounting stress that will inevitably trigger another attack in a few days. The one good thing about it is that at least tomorrow, I know from previous experience, I will be too physically and mentally exhausted to get anything other than a night of deep sleep.

I open my mouth to suck in more air, struggle to expand my chest against the trembling that still wracks me, and exhale again.

It will take another few years to recognize these attacks, this mental siege, and battle for air, for what they are: a symptom of a larger functioning of my brain. When I finally do get a diagnosis of general anxiety disorder, it will come as a relief. *At last*, I think, *I know that I am not just broken.* There is a cause behind this, and I am not the only one to have gone through it. I will breathe easier that night, and from then on, for the most part. The panic attacks never fade entirely, but they do become less frequent and severe, especially when I start admitting that I have them and seek help. I learn to stop fighting the attacks, to let my body go and focus on finding the breath; let my limbs and torso become heavy and sink into the bed like quicksand.

    Eventually, I will find other things that help: medication, counseling, and, completely by accident, Bob Ross. I am in my last semester of grad school when the attacks re-emerge, my body shakes and I again fight for deep, fulfilling breath that will help usher in new calm. One night, I will wander out to my living room, flop down on the couch and turn on the TV on a whim in hopes of distracting my brain until my body exhausts itself again and I can go back to sleep. I will pick an episode of Joy of Painting on Netflix to see if it will do anything to help. The artist loads his palette with paint and sets to work on a blank canvas.
    "We don't make mistakes. We just have happy accidents," Bob intones. By the end of the episode, I am struggling to stay awake.
    One day I will find more things that soothe the trembling and return my breath: the soft fur of a cat, stoically bestowing his affections on me without prompting; the soft noises accompanying the sleepy rise and fall of breaths from someone close and dearly beloved next to me in the familiar, comforting dark.
    Back in my dorm room, years away from any of those things, I finally manage to pull a deep draft of air into my lungs and the

Finding Breath

tremors still for a moment. Another wave hits, but I counter it with another deep breath. On and on the cycle repeats, gaining traction over the spasms at last. The mini fridge hums, the increased air to my brain calms, and I close my eyes and focus on the beach in my mind. I follow my breath, syncing it with the lap of the waves in my head, following them all towards sleep.

The Breaking of Air
Steven Torriano Berry

It was a world where culture meant everything...a world where truth, honor and strict discipline ruled. It was a world with no war, no fear, no hate and no animosity. In this place, 'Peace' was cherished, abundant, and ever flowing...like air.

In this world was a rebellious child, a bright child—a brilliant child. A child who prized his independence, thought for himself, questioned his culture, and one day disobeyed the rules. His crime was simple enough, but of great magnitude, and considered very serious.

In this culture it was mandatory that when greeting someone for the very first time it must be a memorable event marked by a great roar to break the air, followed by the brandishing of sharp talons and a flashy display of long, jagged, gut-ripping teeth. The ferocity must be so intense and heartfelt that nothing remained that could ever be used in the future as a source of hate, anger, or aggression. Due to the great effectiveness of this "Greeting Purge," there had not been one fight, argument, or disagreement amongst the populations on Navija'e Prime 4 in many Galactons. And, its citizens were prosperous, happy, and very well behaved.

It all started one day when Komongo was introduced to his parents' Work Overlord for the very first time, and he hardly let out a growl. It was a major show of disrespect that brought great shame and embarrassment upon his family. Word spread rapidly throughout the Lanzion Scour District that something had to be done. After a hastily conducted hearing by the Prime Lords of the Judi'este, it was ruled that as punishment, Komongo was to be banished from the Scour into the Neverlands. This was a vast wasteland in the dry, vacant Zuma Region, far from civilization. While there, he was to think about his crime, ponder over what he had done wrong, and contemplate the reasons he failed to break the air.

The next day, with no indication of when or if he could ever return, he was escorted far out into the wasteland and left there all alone. Komongo did not like the Neverlands. It was too quiet, too peaceful, and too serene. In the city there was the abundant clamor of life. The great roars of greeting that hung thick in the air, like dense clouds of rage, soothing the mind, and reassuring the soul. Amongst the civic clamor of noise and rolling waves of oral uproar, there was no doubt that you were in the world and of the world, but this? This was real punishment. It was cruel, harsh, and unyielding. It was meant to teach a lesson Komongo had already learned. He knew he was wrong. He regretted it now. And, he would never, ever do it again.

Time passed slowly as the twin suns of Ziroas arose and fell above him. Day after day, the air was hot and scorching as Komongo replayed his crime in his head over and over again, so many times he could have gone blind. At night, with his eyes closed, and the chill eating away at his cartilage, he would re-dream the fateful incident. At the time he was tired and hungry, and did not want to meet his parent's mean, old, ugly Work Overlord anyway. They never had anything nice to say about him, so why should he care? Other than the fact that it was what was expected of him, and the fact that it was… his culture.

Galacton after boring galacton, Komongo endured the searing heat, the freezing nights, the barren landscape and the torturous silence. He kept waiting, hoping and praying for the day when he would be retrieved, forgiven, and allowed to go home. As more time passed, he began to miss his mother and his father tremendously. He missed his friends, his schooling, and he missed the fun of playing with his pet Gola'bo. He began to feel like he had been forgotten, and his sentence would never end, when one day he heard a shrill, crackling sound high above him. He looked up and saw a shining object streaking across the bright, hazel green sky. It looked like an oblong talon spitting a bright trail of golden light from its tail.

Komongo had never seen anything like it, since nothing on his planet could fly, but he was mesmerized and could not look away as he began to run, moving his scaly, six-jointed tentacles as fast as they could move him. He followed the flying talon, wanting to find out what it was, and where it had come from. A sense of awe and excitement enveloped him, as he realized that, quite likely, he was the only one in the world to have seen it.

The Breaking of Air

As the object landed amongst a thick haze of billowing, dust and debris, Komongo hid himself behind a high-wall of rocks to watch. He gazed at the strange looking thing now sitting quiet and still, hushed against the vast emptiness of the barren landscape. Printed on the side of the Sky Talon was a strange looking symbol he had never seen before. It displayed three odd colors depicting what appeared to be a chaotic series of alternating stripes with stars.

After a long while, an opening appeared at the bottom of the craft, and a long ramp rolled out to settle onto the rocky ground. Several small creatures appeared in the darkened opening. They moved slowly, stopping for a moment as if unsure about taking their next steps, before trudging from the dark to trample down the extended ramp way. Dressed in silvery suits, each carried a funny looking huin'go, or shiny stick cradled within spindly arms. Their heads were covered with large crystal bubbles, but Komongo could still see the hideous masks they must have been wearing beneath. He saw no fur or scales on their faces, and they walked upright on just two, double-jointed tentacles. Komongo ducked back behind the rocks, careful not to be seen. He was scared and for the first time in his life he actually had something to be scared about. He did not like the feeling.

What was this Sky Talon? How could it float and move upon the dense green air like it did? And, what were these alien creatures now crawling about outside its stark, gleaming exterior? When Komongo peeked his head back up to take another look, he saw that two of the small alien creatures were coming toward him. What would he do? Should he run? Should he continue to hide?

Just then, Komongo got an idea. He was being punished for making an improper greeting. This time, he would greet these visitors with great respect, honor his culture, and make up for his earlier crime. The aliens would tell his parents, as well as the Judi'este Lords, what an impressive and powerful greeting they received. He would be praised, forgiven, and allowed to come back home.

As soon as the two aliens were close enough Komongo leapt from his hiding place. He viciously broke the air, honoring them with a loud and mighty ROAR! Then, as his custom demanded, he raised his sharp claws high, mashed his gut-ripping teeth, and let out a terrifying ear-piercing shriek. He was three times their size and he looked and sounded so ferocious. Komongo gave the alien visitors such a 'Greeting Purge' that he just knew they would be pleased.

"LOOK OUT!" one of the sky aliens shouted in an unfamiliar voice. He then raised his huin'go, and fired, as the other one quickly followed suit.

Pain and sharp burning sensations peppered Komongo's body as thick, purple ooze trickled from the wounds. He was being attacked, but why? Once again he was being punished, but this time he had embraced his culture and followed the rules, why were they hurting him?

The Breaking of Air

Other aliens ran up to join in the assault, aiming their fire sticks in a barrage of deadly, flesh piercing rounds. As Komongo fell to the ground, breathless and weak, he began to cry. He was so confused, in so much pain, and it did not make any sense! He had broken the air and made his 'Greeting Purge' with all of his might. It was sincere, heartfelt, and worthy of praise and respect.

As he lay on the ground bleeding out, the assault continued, and the young Karmoidian knew he was about to die. What he did not know was that in the culture of his killers such a vicious greeting was seen as a show of aggression, as an attack. They believed their lives were in danger and they had to protect themselves.

As Komongo's eyes slowly closed for the last time his pain, his confusion, and his desires to go home all faded away.

The small alien creatures cautiously stepped forward, looked down upon the now lifeless inhabitant of this newly "discovered" planet, and reloaded.

Glass Houses
J.E. Brooke

The traveler rolled out of the bed, slowly straightening to ease the lingering stiffness in her back. She stretched in the soft artificial light that filled the room, gradually growing brighter to allow her sleepy eyes to adjust. She took a few steps towards the dresser on the far wall, then looked back to the empty bed out of habit. It still felt too large with just one person. Sometimes she found it hard to sleep with the sense of vacantness, but it had gradually grown a little easier. After today, though, it would no longer be a problem. She finished crossing the room, opened the top dresser drawer and slipped on the one piece of clothing that remained—a long, airy dress with clusters of bright yellow lemons nestled among dark green leaves printed on a background of smooth, blue fabric. Then, she took out the worn knapsack that had been beside the dress and put it on top of the dresser.

Everything she wanted to bring with her was inside: a change of clothes (just in case), framed pictures of her children, a friction-worn stone from her favorite walking path. All the things she had wanted to keep with her until the very end of her days here, and had not already been sent ahead with the rest of her belongings. The room had once been vibrant, pictures and paintings she had done filling up the smooth white walls, giving the small space some personality and life. They had all been taken down and moved over the last few days in preparation for her departure and, tomorrow, someone new would make the space their own. The thought made her a little sad, but this day was an inevitability. Someone else would need it more now, she told herself. Not allowing herself to look back, the traveler picked up her bag and walked out the door. It automatically closed behind her.

The dormitory halls were silent, everyone else at work or school or nursery, depending on their age. The light blue paint on the walls was pristine, well-kept, and helped to soften the lack of noise and turn the silence soothing. Doorways opened onto rec rooms, cafeterias, libraries—all empty and waiting for the people to return after their daily engagements. This building which had been her home was so full of life in the evenings. She wished she didn't have to leave in the middle of the day. But it could not be helped, or avoided, and the traveler's husband might already be waiting for her outside. The possibility gave her the proper motivation to step forward. There was another automatic door, a rush of air, and her eyes squinted against the sudden sunlight.

The air all around was quiet, except for a few singing birds in a nearby tree. The paved path leading from the immaculate whitewashed dormitory was lined with bursts of bright tropical flowers. The red, yellow, and purple blossoms now seemed gathered in a processional announcing her departure. She knew, though, there was no cause for such a distinction. She needed to be on her way. Walking away from the building, her thoughts turned to what lay outside. Would her husband really be there waiting for her by the main gate? She wouldn't be hurt (she hoped) if he hadn't been able to walk with her to the new house. She knew he had duties to perform at work, duties that she would have to fulfill soon enough when she began her own assignment in a few days.

As she followed the path away from the dormitories, the lush blooms she passed were larger, closer together, until at last they became a chaotic thicket of life and beauty. Individuals indistinguishable from the whole. She smiled. A fitting metaphor for her life here. Long ago, whole societies would have balked and rioted at such a notion, but then again, for them, this way of life had not been necessary. They had had the luxury of choice, and look where that had gotten them. Her world was left to deal with the consequences, and all things considered, the solution wasn't that bad in the grand scheme of things. The traveler lifted her gaze from the attractive blooms and deep green leaves upward to the treetops overhead as they lifted their branches. They were carefully pruned by the residents assigned to care for them, but some of the leaves were rebelliously close to pressing up against the glass of the dome that separated them from the outside world.

Through some of the sparser branches, the faded rust-brown and concrete-gray of the city skyline loomed over the dome glass. She gulped reflexively. Not that she was afraid to go to the city (not really). Her ancestors had been taken from among its inhabitants, after all. It's just that it would be so different, compared to living her life here. The traveler was suddenly aware that her breath was quickening out of control, her diaphragm tightening and the world beginning to spin in response. Frustrated by her own physiological fear response, she forced herself to stop walking and breathe deeply, expanding and contracting the muscles trying to strangle her guts, as she repeated the mantra everyone living within the confines of the dome was taught. In a soothing rhythm, she remembered the words: *They did it for us, for our children, and all the generations after. Even after I am gone, Humanity will continue. Because of me, it will thrive.*

Not a particularly catchy slogan, but it had been inside her head all the same from when she was a small child, repeating after her mother and father in their family dormitory. Many years after her parents had left for the outside, she herself had listened to scores of children recite it as they cycled through her classroom, up through the levels until they inherited posts of their own in the ecosystem. Catchy or not, the worn familiarity of it was as much an anchor to the physical world as the stone she carried in her knapsack, and her calm returned.

The traveler resumed moving forward, more slowly this time. Every step took her closer to the main exit of the dome, the end of her old life in paradise and the beginning of her new one in the world outside. She stopped occasionally along the thickly gardened path, not from fear or panic but from a pure desire to savor her last moments in the lush, beautiful environs she had always known. There would be no chance to see them again once she passed through the final doors. She knew the history of the domes and their many fail-safes too well, had taught it too many times to believe otherwise. She could still recite the lesson without needing a reference, had repeated it last to the young educator assigned to replace her.

The retiring lecturer and her replacement stood alone in the strangely quiet classroom. The students had all gone, but evidence of their presence remained in the form of bright, colorful construction paper cutouts and stick-figure drawings on the walls next to the lecturer's own paintings. A final contribution to her class. The trash bin in the corner was stuffed full of dirty disposable plates, streaked with crusted lines of blue icing and stray cake crumbs. A special treat for her last day. The protégée had been carefully selected and groomed for this, just as she had been. The trainee completed months of observation in class, an opportunity for her to learn about the students and practice her interactions with them but also a chance for the lecturer herself to watch for signs of trouble: hints of dissent, inappropriate or troublesome questions. Such things had still been known to manifest, even at this late stage of cultivation, and needed to be purged immediately if detected. But thus far she had seen no such troubling symptoms in her apprentice, and she smiled with pride before beginning her last lesson.

Rumors swirled within the dome of other ways of passing along information from one person to another, but the executors had ruled that rote memorization was still the only acceptable method for training new lecturers.

Glass Houses

Otherwise, there was too much deviation from the official narrative of history, too much room for other narratives to creep in and contaminate the placid contentedness of the ecosystem. The lecturer began:

"Before the domes there was sickness and suffering. There could never be enough domes to shelter all of humanity, of course, but with them, at least some of the people might be spared. When the contaminant first appeared, no one knew the danger it represented. Adults who contracted it were usually fine. A very few died, but those people were usually sick from before. It wasn't until children were born to the infected parents that they knew. And then, oh, how they knew. Such children that were born! The contaminant spread, carried on gossamer wings and a stinging, itching bite as it followed a radically changing climate. Eventually, the domes were devised as a solution to preserve enough of humanity that the wellspring would remain pure—"

"Ma'am," the trainee interrupted. The lecturer's eyes flew open. This was an unexpected development, but this would be the last chance her pupil had to question the executors' narrative without punishment. The only chance of correction. "Didn't they try anything else before they built the domes? I've read about things in the archives: vaccines and antivirals. Help and support for the children who were born affected by the contaminant. Why didn't they try those first?"

"It is not our place to ask why," the lecturer replied smoothly and with confidence, the correct response. She neglected to mention that she herself once had such doubts when first starting her vocation, although she wisely kept them to herself until they faded. Once, she wondered what might have happened if the people of the past had not been so obsessed with walls and barriers, if they put stock in other solutions instead. But that was not what had happened, and it had been years since she had wondered anything of the kind. "We live in the time that they created for us, as they intended. There is no higher way of honoring the original executors than continuing on that path." She paused, waiting to see if the younger woman had any more questions. The trainee stayed silent, so the lecturer continued.

"The first domes were not without their problems, of course, as the brave men and women who built them were as human as we are. The wrong kind of glass was used or faulty environmental control systems failed, and the inhabitants starved or ran out of water or were boiled alive. (There had been more than a few distasteful jokes about what came from building glass houses, but the lecturer didn't mention it.) Or they were set upon or sabotaged by angry mobs of the incompatible, those who were already infected or designated unsuitable for other reasons by the original executors. It could not be helped that more resources were diverted to those who went within the domes, but those who remained on the outside would never understand the sacrifice those in the domes made. To seal themselves off from the outside world, even if they had better food and more beautiful things to look at, to sacrifice of themselves for the sake of humanity, how could those on the outside ever hope to understand that those resources were earned? But they did not understand, and they grew angry, and there were unfortunate attacks until solutions were devised by the executors in their enterprising benevolence."

The lecturer chanced a look at her trainee, expecting to see the usual pride at the executors' cleverness and ingenuity that usually filled her students' faces at this point in the lesson, but saw something entirely different. And more troubling. The trainee frowned mildly, possessed by an apparently stubborn sour thought.

"What is it?" the lecturer asked.

"I just thought," the trainee replied, chewing her lip nervously while she paused. "I wondered if the outsiders have ever heard our narrative before. And if they might see things differently than we do."

The lecturer's own brow creased deeply. "We do not ask these questions. They are not our concern, nor are they useful. Questions like this only cause discomfort and upset in the present, they cannot fix or change the past or give us insight into the future. You will not ask a question like that again."

"But I only—"

"If you let these doubts continue and speak them aloud, you won't live long enough to see the outside. You will be identified as a contaminant yourself and destroyed as such. Is that what you want?"

The lecturer's sudden flare of anger ebbed as she saw her trainee on the verge of tears. She took a step closer to the other woman and cautiously laid a hand on her shoulder in a gesture of comfort.

"Please don't think that I'm telling you this because I don't care about you," the lecturer said quietly. "Quite the opposite, actually. I've become fond of you during your training, and I think you have great promise. You will help prepare our young ones for their lives here, and then outside, but you can't do that if you are designated a threat to our way of life."

There was still hurt in the younger woman's eyes, but she stayed silent.

Satisfied, the lecturer resumed:

"The barriers were installed well away from the dome wall to prevent the incompatible from making further attacks, and the incompatible were increasingly monitored to prevent and pacify any future attempts at disruption. Faulty equipment was replaced and functional equipment was kept in working order with automated maintenance. And as a compromise to the incompatible, the compatible born within the domes would only be allowed to stay until their fiftieth year, after they have birthed and raised the new generation. The only exception were the executors, of course, but that could not be helped. Someone needed to be preserved to lead."

Done with the narrative, the lecturer waited for the appropriate reaction from her protégée, which was, of course, respectful silence. The two women wasted no time with goodbyes. There would be a time for that later at her farewell that evening, when everyone in the ecosystem gathered to celebrate her time in the dome. Instead, the lecturer left her successor to survey the classroom, and make any necessary adjustments before she took over the next day.

    The traveler caught a glimpse of the exit through a gap in the lush hanging wall of orchids and violets, a lone passage jutting from the outer surface of the dome, sealed at the glass wall and the final exit by two sturdy metal doors. Maintenance crews in dirt-stained denim overalls tended the flower beds, vegetable patches, and fruit trees not too far from the exitway; picking, pruning and pollinating wherever they were needed. All younger people, some of whom she had taught, most of whom she would probably never see again. She left the overhanging passage of trellised lilies and orchids, their scent lingering for the first few steps back onto the open path, and walked the rest of the way to the exit.
    Distorted into blurry waves by the thick glass, she thought she could just make out a small crowd on the other side of the electrified perimeter. Was her husband among them, waiting to take her to their home outside? She looked forward to that, getting settled in and making it her own. Making it theirs, at last. It wouldn't be like within the dome, (how could it be?), but it would at least be a comfortable place to live out the rest of her life. Decent food, good bed nets, limited climate control, and sealed windows. It was better than what

those who had been born on the outside had, but then, after all the residents of the domes had sacrificed and grown used to, former insiders like herself couldn't be expected to go without entirely. The executors couldn't just leave her with nothing. It wouldn't be fair.

The traveler approached the door, coming within range of its sensor at last. It knew her and slid open with a mildly grating woosh. She stepped through, into the glass corridor, and the door wooshed behind her again, the grating becoming a bone-rattling grind as it suddenly halted on its track. The door had closed most of the way, but there was still a three or four inch gap between the door and the glass wall. It allowed her an extra glance into the environment that had been her home, her whole world, for fifty years. She should call to the maintenance crew about the door so they could come over and fix it, sealing her off for good, but suddenly she was hungry for more time. Telling them to fix something so small wasn't her responsibility anymore, and how could they deprive her of this? But the second door was already opening ahead of her. She froze. There was cool, conditioned air caressing her front even as humid, swampy air rushed in from the outside along with the late morning heat. Her eyes watered in response and she squeezed them shut. She wiped away the moisture, reopened her eyes, and walked forward until she was halfway through the door, with one foot on either side of the track.

She knew she should keep moving, had been instructed not to stop for any reason until the second door was sealed behind her so that there would be no possibility of a breach, but she was sure that something as insignificant as a backward glance wouldn't cause much harm. Claiming the moment for herself and everything she had contributed in her life, she stopped in the open doorway and cast one last look back through the crack in the first door, longing for it even now. The traveler didn't even notice the high buzzing sound of gossamer-fine wings going past her, bearing the minute body that controlled them- full of vital blood and precious eggs-into the open passage and through the gap to explore a world it had never seen before. The contaminant found a puddle made by one of the maintenance crew watering the garden, and began to lay her eggs in the stagnant water.

Unaware and unbothered, the traveler took the next step through the door, craning her neck, trying to pick her husband out from among the crowd.

The Breath
Laura Goldman Weinberg

> Your grace rides on the crest
>
> Of the wave of the breath
>
>
>
> The breath
>
> The ocean of consciousness
>
> That permeates and joins the worlds
>
>
>
> Like the strings of a kite
>
> Pulling and stretching
>
> Going higher and higher
>
>
>
> The breath
>
> Reaches into the cosmos
>
> And pulls in Your grace and love
>
> And offers it back out to You

The Breath

It's the breath

That is the dance

And the dancer

The breath

Leads and sways

Pulls and lets go

The breath

Is the cosmic love

The cosmic lover

How divine

How gracious

How glorious

How simple

How profound

Writers of the Aether

Something so simple

That everyone on earth has

Yet do they know

What a gift it is

Sink into the breath

Enjoy the mysteries of life

Your love

The greatest mystery

The greatest gift

Is Your love

The Butterfly, the Tornado, and the Sailboat
Derek Maurer

Jerry and I gazed at a slight rustling high above. A few backlit leaves, glowing green against the summer sky, waved slowly, resignedly. It was stupefyingly hot that afternoon, suffocatingly humid; the wind refused even to purse its lips to blow, and the smoke from Jerry's cigarette rose straight up. But those leaves, that errant breeze we could not feel. We kept watching.

This was in the ravine across from Jerry's parents' house, where we would go to smoke pot and range through the timbered reserve. We would stop at a particular log on the way in and light up, inhaling the inspiration for our tales, fantasies, and wild speculations. He was the first one to teach me birds, the different kinds and their different calls. Or, as on this day looking up through the branches and the shadows and shafts of sunlight, we might be taken with something random, like the breeze that browsed quietly overhead, rustling a few leaves here and a few leaves there, then resting and reappearing somewhere else. In my mind the scene is better with the piping of bluejays echoing through the gallery of trees, so let's make that stipulation, whether it was exactly so or not.

We both read Carlos Castaneda in those days, Jerry and I, and we talked about it often. We were ready to believe, or at least pretend, some supernatural force was at play in the woods, that the breeze had volition or was moved by an unseen hand, the work of a sorcerer, maybe, like in the books. It was fun to think about it. And I thought about it again years later, reading an article on the Butterfly Effect. That's the notion that a butterfly's wings flapping in Brazil might eventually steer a tornado in Texas, and though it's commonplace now, back then chaos theory was a novelty outside of mathematics symposia. I don't know how it came to Newsweek's attention, and I don't remember anything else about the article, just the butterfly and the tornado.

As Wikipedia notes concerning the Butterfly Effect: "Although a butterfly flapping its wings has remained constant in the expression of this concept, the location of the butterfly, the consequences, and the location of the consequences have varied widely."[1] Well, that leaves such a lot of room for the imagination.

Our lake has a bad reputation among sailors. They don't like the fickle breezes, calling them "puffy and shifty." I've repeated the slander many times, but not anymore.

I do understand where the notion came from. We all have our stories, the times a sudden gust or shift nearly capsized us, or did, or left us hanging out over the lee side of the boat. The wind likes to mess with you precisely when you are in the middle of a maneuver, when the forces are shifting from one side to the other; that is to say, when you are most vulnerable. It happens plenty out there. It is confounding and unpredictable, but not unfathomable. Here is what I have come to

The Butterfly, the Tornado, and the Sailboat

understand: The wind bends and rolls and turns. It bunches up and it spreads out.

The weather forecast tells you it will be from the northwest today at such-and-such a speed, and that's what you picture: a northwest breeze moving in a straight line. It may be so above the trees, but on our lake, on the South Arm where we sail, that northwest breeze will have dipped down to run the channel between the North and South arms, ridden up over Cottage Reserve, and dived over the trees on the north shore by the time it reaches us. And as it pours from the shoreline to the water it sprays out (like a cow pissing on a flat rock, the farm kids at school used to say), creating turbulence that is difficult to read in your sails. They have air in them one moment and none the next. Then too, some of this northwest breeze finds its way through the narrows west of our cove, forming a current flowing eastward, which then interacts with the prevailing wind to create yet more turbulence. It's why, I think, we often note two or more distinct wave patterns in the water.

If we could just see the air, what a mess it would be of currents and eddies and cross-currents amid shorelines like dams, trees like snow fences, narrows like funnels, and inlets like alleyways where wind-blown trash collects. But we can't see air, only its indications—ripples on the water, the flag that flies across from our dock, how the other boats have their sails trimmed.

When they complain about our puffy and shifty winds, what they mean is they want predictability. They want to set a course and not have to change it. They want west to be west and north to be north. There are places you can have all that. I've been to some of them and liked it a lot. But our lake is our lake and this is where we live. To wish otherwise would be to want a different life, and I don't feel like starting over at this point. I'll cast my lot with puffy and shifty. I'll watch the sails, jib and main, and feel the tug of the sheets, ready to trim in or out any moment, ready to steer and to jump to port or starboard as need demands. Alacrity will be my hallmark as my mind's eye shows me the jets blasting from the narrows and the curlicues winding along the shore. The wind's every change will be my teacher, and when I am confounded I will take it as my emblem and my cause to look within and not without. And if I ever have two sailboats of my own, I will name them Puffy and Shifty.

These insights cost me years of bumbling around the lake with false notions about the nature of moving air. Air bends, and all we sailors do is bend it with flaps of sailcloth to make the boat go. It's only in the past few summers I've begun to feel confident in my new beliefs about the wind, about our lake, about how to make a sailboat go where you want it to go. I was looking forward to the season, eager to start lessons, excited to observe conditions and test my ideas, when Covid hit.

A few weeks in, a sailing friend wrote to ask how I was doing with the loss of the season, and I never answered his e-mail. I

The Butterfly, the Tornado, and the Sailboat

couldn't figure out how I was doing with it. There was so much to grieve and who was I to pine over a pastime? What else had we lost, even then? The ability to gather, if we were smart. Any sense of common purpose in nation or state. The illusion that we were a society bending, however slowly, toward Justice.

Tiny perturbations, extreme and unpredictable consequences. Droplets so small you'd never notice them, borne through the air from my lungs to yours. You're welcome. Eight-and-a-half minutes of video that begged the question, What do the words, "I can't breathe," mean coming from a Black man's lips? It's as if that butterfly steered the tornado right into our house. It ripped away the roof and now we have to look at all our stuff in the unsparing daylight, mostly as it was before everything changed. It turns out we have a mess on our hands. There's trash everywhere and definite signs of abuse in the home; we've blown through our savings and inheritance and we're pretty much broke. Now fights are breaking out.

It must be our turn in history's maelstrom, where everything swirls and there's no telling how far away it will land. If we could see through time, see the chains of events unfolding, what a mess it would be of causes and effects and counter-effects, of reactions and reactions to reactions. Who has that kind of sight? Mostly, we make do with indications—the mask-wearing, the voting by mail; the sun setting in an orange haze, the lines down and power out for a week; the stark facts of privilege and the unanswerable questions about the fate of the Republic. All I can say is, Watch your sails, friends, watch the water. Keep your hand on the tiller and be ready to jump.

What a light these days cast on former times when events did not spin so furiously. A long-lost friend in a cathedral of trees, leaves like stained glass; the smell of a cigarette, the bluejays' piercing call; the barest whisper of a breeze, not able or not willing to tell what would befall.

[1] Wikipedia, the Free Encyclopedia, n.v. "Butterfly Effect," (accessed Nov. 30, 2020), https://en.wikipedia.org/wiki/Butterfly_effect.

Also Check Out
THE WRITERS' ROOMS

the writers' rooms
www.TheWritersRooms.org

OUR ROOTS
The Writers' Rooms began in late 2015 under the welcoming umbrella of the Iowa Writers' House. We had a simple mission in mind: create a free, accessible community to Iowan writers. The Violet Realm, our sci-fi/fantasy Room, started it all. For two years we incubated under the IWH and learned what our community needed to foster creative minds. It became apparent that if we were going to support our writers, it would be through a community- and crowd-sourced endeavor.

OUR MISSION

Our writing community has the amazing benefit of a massive collection of backgrounds, experiences, and viewpoints. The Writers' Rooms endeavors to bring these wonderful ideas together and help all writers with their craft. We strive to encourage and foster community-based knowledge to help lead literary sessions and provide a safe, positive writing environment. Our Rooms are moderated by both our Concierges and the members of our community. Community-led sessions tap into the wealth of our collective knowledge, allowing our writers to both share their own experiences and learn from other attendees.

The Rooms can't exist without you and your passion and experience!

OUR PEOPLE

Concierge members come from the writing community. All of our current concierges were interested in their topics and became knowledgeable about their genre through reading, writing, and taking lessons of their own. Anyone interested in leading a particular genre- or topic-based Room is welcome to e-mail us at welcome@thewritersrooms.org.

The rest of the Room membership comes from eager writer minds who want to know more about a particular genre or topic. Some have even graciously led lessons for us. We're always looking for more people to share their expertise.

Find out more at: Facebook (IAWritersRooms), and follow us on Instagram (@WritersRooms) and Twitter (@IAWritersRooms).

www.ingramcontent.com/pod-product-compliance
Lightning Source LLC
Chambersburg PA
CBHW022022290426
44109CB00015B/1274